Down Memory Lane
in Retford
1925- 1950

EAST RETFORD CHURCH FROM THE AIR

Edited by
Angela Meads

Published by
Bookworm of Retford
Spa Lane, Retford, Nottinghamshire. DN22 7PB
01777 869224

ISBN 0955167418
978-0955167416

First printed 2006

Printed and bound by
Burgess Photo Print Ltd
Beehive Street, Retford.

CONTENTS

Acknowledgements

I would like to thank the following Retfordians who have shared their memories with me.

George Roberts	Raymond Butler
June Smith	Fred Pimperton
Muriel Ogle	Cynthia Cockayne
Ernest Widdowson	Doug Davison
Ken Sturgess	Vic Hall
Keith Smith	Arthur Sanderson
Harry Wilson	Thelma Larkinson
Valerie Davis	Margaret Morrell
Mr Pearson	Roseen Butler
Mr J. Jones	

Thank you to many other residents of the town that enthusiastically helped verify information.

Technical help has been gratefully received from
Paul Meads, Leah Meads, Katie Meads,
Paul Jones and Bob Burgess
Bassetlaw Museum

> **'I tend to live in the past because most of my life is there.'**
>
> *Herb Caen, 1916-1997*

At Home

The way of life in Thrumpton and Ordsall in the 1930s had changed little since the previous century. It was common in those days for families with a yard or garden to own one or two pigs and some chickens. The houses on Jubilee Terrace (just off Brecks Road) were built with space for a pig, chickens and a vegetable plot. The land which belonged to the homes on Jubilee Terrace, once used for the family pig, the wash-house, outdoor toilet and long garden is now the site of a wide road and newer housing. When these houses were built there were no roads, just pathways and the path at the front of the houses still remains.

Rearing a pig in the back garden was a shared community exercise. Not everyone wanted to keep a pig and some people simply had no room so they would get involved with the raising of a friends or neighbours pig by saving scraps of food to add to the pig-swill bucket.

Jubilee Terrace, now known as Brecks Road

The killing of the pig was also a shared event and news would go round the neighbourhood that a pig was ready for the table. Crowds of excited children would come running; daring each other to watch. At one particular home on Brecks Road the tricky business of killing the pig was performed by an engine driver from Century Road! He had no previous butchery experience but he was willing and skilful.

George Roberts, born at All Hallows Cottage, Thrumpton, remembers his family having a pig. When it was time to preserve the bacon, he would be sent to Gladish's shop (at the corner of Albert Road and Carolgate) to buy a block of salt. This was then broken up into fine pieces by bashing it with a rolling pin. Once the joints of ham, bacon and sausages had been made, gifts of meat would be handed out to the neighbours that had helped raise the pig.

Each morning, many children would be sent to the local dairy farmer before school with a jug to get some fresh milk for breakfast, but milk was also delivered by horse and cart and was sold directly from the milk churn. On Century Road in the 1940s, milk was delivered in this way by a dairy woman called Olive Thompson.

Girl collecting milk. 1920s (Welchman Collection)

Cynthia Cockayne was born in 1933 in a cottage on Burkett's Row on the High Street, Ordsall (now demolished). It was one of three terraced cottages and was so small that the only upstairs bedroom was reached via a ladder. Cynthia spent a happy childhood playing in the streets and lanes of Ordsall which were safe from traffic, though not from the daily procession of cows on their way to the milking sheds, leaving a trail of cow muck along the roads.

Ordsall Carnival Queen 1950

(C. Cockayne)

A chapel on the High Street provided much of Cynthia's social life and 3d (about 2p) was eagerly paid to see a magic lantern show there, showing pictures of the Holy Land. Cynthia remembers thinking how beautiful those far away places looked and how warm the weather, compared to her home village.

Happy days were spent with Miss Thompson and Miss Burton at Ordsall Infant School and there was great excitement when Father Christmas came to give out apples, oranges, a book or a skipping rope.

As a child, Cynthia loved playing at being a shopkeeper and she remembers getting a shopkeepers till for Christmas and a bus conductor's ticket set.

Summer carnivals took place in many parts of the town. Horses and drays were decorated with streamers and ribbons and Cynthia was proudly crowned Carnival Queen at the Ordsall Carnival and rode through the village on a decorated coal lorry.

Tea in Ordsall Village Hall with Cynthia Cockayne as Carnival Queen seated on the right, 1950.

(C. Cockayne)

Hallcroft Carnival 1939   *(Welchman)*

The General Strike of 1926 affected Retford families in the same way as it affected the rest of the nation. The strike, in support of the coalminers, (who had refused to accept a reduction in wages) lasted 10 days, but this was long enough to leave families penniless by the end of the first week. In Retford, the Salvation Army, on Exchange Street, provided a soup kitchen for those in need.

The pawnbroker's shop, at 19 Carolgate, was open for trade and was especially busy during the week of the strike. The three arms of the old pawnbroker's sign can still be seen on the side of the building that was known later, for many years, as Barker's the greengrocer and more recently as Ponden Mills.

The prospect of hardship was a constant worry to many families, so membership to a 'friendly society' was a popular option. The Independent Order of the Rechabites, (founded 1835) was available in Retford and meetings were held in the chapel on Carolgate. This was a teetotal organisation and a few pence each week was paid by members into the society's funds. In return, financial help would be given in times of sickness or unemployment, but not necessarily to unmarried mothers or to those that strayed into the drinking houses. Before the introduction of National Insurance in 1911, the workhouse would have been the only option to the destitute. At first, the National Insurance only covered working men and women, not their families, so friendly societies were still favourable.

The Rechabite Club in Retford provided a social life for members too, with free trips to Cleethorpes by rail. Children would hurry home from school to catch the 4pm train with their families.

Teatime was spent on the beach, eating sandwiches brought from home. After a few games on the sand, there would be just enough time to buy a stick of rock before catching the train home again. In the school holidays, a train would be specially commissioned by the society and a whole day at the seaside was the highlight of the year for many children.

Decorative membership card from about 1920.

The remains of the bracket of the pawnbroker's sign can still be seen on the side of the building at 19 Carolgate.

In the 1930s, market day was Saturday, with farmers' fairs in March and October. The March fair was primarily for horses, cattle and cheese and the October fair originally sold hops, wool, sheep and cattle. The stacks of cheeses were placed on straw in Cannon Square with hops and wool piled high on carts, but by the 1930s, the farmers' participation was dwindling and being replaced by the fun fair that we know today.

Dusty roads in the town were dampened down by water carts, spraying water from behind. Children loved to follow the carts and run in and out of the spray. Road sweepers kept the crossing free from horse and cow dung.

Riding a bicycle without a light after dark was a serious offence and a local policeman could fine a person four shillings (20p) in 1930. It may not sound much now, but a 15 year old would earn less than 50p per week.

A Complete Pawnbroker's Sign

A Special Parcel

Five year old Fred Pimperton, on his way to the Council School in Thrumpton in 1923, had to wait at the level crossing for the gates to open as rail workers were laying new lines. The foreman spotted little Fred looking through the gates and was reminded of his own grandson who had recently grown out of a smart woollen suit. The foreman told Fred that if he were at the crossing in the morning he would give him the suit.

Fred did not own a suit or even a jacket, so he made sure he was there the next day. As promised, he was given a parcel tied up with string, which he carried to school and back.

The parcel was opened at home to reveal a striking chequered suit which he proudly wore for the photograph opposite.

The house in the background is 103 Thrumpton Lane, later demolished and replaced with the offices of the Northern Rubber Company.

'Mid pleasures and palaces though we may roam
Be it ever so humble, there's no place like home'

John Howard Payne (1791-1852)

Fred Pimperton (bottom row, far right) outside his home, about 1922.

(F. Pimperton)

FUN, GAMES AND PASTIMES

The Majestic Theatre was built in 1927 and the building contractors were Richmond and Sons of Retford. Richmond and Sons were responsible for many other buildings and bridges in the town such as Grove Street Bridge, Loesby's outfitters (the building now occupied by Bacon's the butchers), the Picture House, Cyril Getliffe's café and his Billiard Hall on Carolgate. Richmond and Sons had offices and a joinery yard on West Street. The architect for the Majestic was Alfred Thraves of Nottingham.

The silent films of the 1920s were a great incentive for children to learn to read. The action of the Cowboys and Indians could only be fully enjoyed by reading the captions at the bottom of the screen. The films may have been silent, but the excited young audience, in the Saturday 'tuppeny rush', was certainly not, as the captions were often read out loud.

The Picture Palace, next to Carolgate Bridge, was converted in 1930 from a building previously used as a roller skating rink. It was known as the Olympia rink, but only one year after opening, Cyril Getliffe converted it to a cinema; such was the demand for the silent movie.

The Majestic Theatre, Coronation Street 2005

A Saturday afternoon show for youngsters would cost about 2d (about 1p). In the evening, dating couples had the added comfort of double seats in the back row!

In 1930, the Retford Times reported the following:

"Mr Cyril Getliffe, the well known amusement caterer has converted, at great expense, the former Olympia Rink near Carolgate Bridge, into one of the most convenient and up to-date picture palaces in the country. It has been fitted up and decorated in fine style, and there will be comfortable seating accommodation for 600 persons... The National Gas Engine Co. have installed one of their latest type 18.5 horsepower gas engines for the purpose of generating the electric light."

Two Teenagers 1949

'We went regularly to all three cinemas in Retford, the Ritz, Roxy and the Majestic. I can remember going to watch films starring Fred Astaire and Ginger Rogers. There were westerns about Jesse James and we watched Orson Wells starring in the *'Third Man'*. Sometimes we bought a drink in the café at the Roxy.

"God Save the King" was always played at the end of a film. Me and my friends would jump up quickly out of our seats before the National Anthem started. Sometimes we would be watching the clock so that we could nip out of the cinema before 10'o'clock to give us time to place a last order for a drink in the "Criterion" pub. It closed at 10pm.'

Doug Davison

'I was only 11 years old in 1927, when the Majestic Theatre was built by Mr Getliffe. Me and my friends would go round to Coronation Street after school or at the weekend to watch the builders. We knew it was going to be a really big special theatre. I can remember that the first show was *'No, No, Nanette'*, but I never went to see it; it would have seemed expensive in those days.

When I was a bit older, about 14 years old, my best friend was the son of the owner of the Newcastle Arms on Bridgegate. This was a bit of luck because this pub was where the dancing girls boarded when they were putting on a show at the Majestic. The girls were only teenagers themselves and we would spend the evening chatting to them.'

Doug Davison

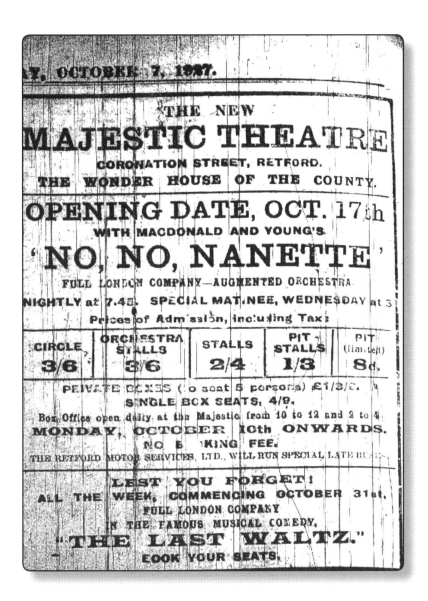

An advertisement from the Retford Times proclaiming the
grand opening of the Majestic Theatre 1927

Towards the end of the Second world War, the Ritz was sold to the Corporation and was used to store grain. Seats were removed to make more space for storage and the cinema did not reopen again, so some of the seats were used to replace ones at the Roxy on Carolgate. The last film to be shown at the Ritz was *'King Kong'*.

During 1944 a film called *'None Shall Escape'* was shown at the Majestic. To advertise the show, workers from the Majestic dressed up in German and Home Guard uniforms and stood on the steps of the cinema, showing the Home Guard soldier holding the German airman and sailor at gunpoint.

Attendance at the two cinemas was already running down by the late 1940s, so to save money, the popular newsreel was shared between the Roxy and the Majestic, with a runner taking it from one to the other each evening.

Keith Smith

'During the first year or two of World War Two, I belonged to an Amateur Dramatic Society that was formed from people that attended St Michael's church. The aim of the society was to put on weekly entertainment. Sometimes this would be films starring Laurel and Hardy or Buster Keaton. We put on nativity plays at Christmas and variety shows at other times. The shows were staged on the small stage in the church hall. We were all really enthusiastic and we wanted to make the shows look more professional by getting some better lighting and curtains.

To raise the money we held dances at the Town Hall on a Wednesday and Friday. We weren't usually able to get Harry Clarke and his band as he was in high demand, but Cyril Coupe and his band usually played for us and they were also very good.

The Town Hall was always packed, especially with military men, who were staying at the local army camps. There were no refreshments in the Town Hall so when people got thirsty, they would nip out to the Half Moon. They were given a pass so that they could get back into the dance.

 Some nights were a bit lively in the town centre, especially in Cannon Square. Rival groups of soldiers would sometimes start fighting. These groups were in The Vine and The Crown. One night I saw a fight going on in the Crown and someone was pushed right through the window. The military police came along to sort it all out.'

Keith Smith

One of eight wall mounted mermaids in the Majestic Theatre.

Fred Pimperton 1927

'I used to go to the Picture Palace, near Carolgate Bridge, on a Saturday morning with friends. It would cost 2d to sit on the wooden forms at the front.

When a group of young lads got together there was usually a bit of mischief going on, such as sticking gum to the bench ready for the next person to sit on. Many of the lads, like me, were still in short trousers, so gum would end up on the back of our legs! My favourite films starred Charlie Chaplin or Buster Keaton and of course Laurel and Hardy and I liked the cowboy films. Sometimes a pianist would play to accompany the silent film and the lads would shout out things to him. It was usually to tell him what was going to happen next in the film or maybe to try to put him off his playing!

If I had enough money for sweets to take into the film, I would buy a small bar of Cadbury's Chocolate for 1d or some aniseed balls. We usually went in the little sweet shop at the end of New Street.'

Fred Pimperton

June Smith 1940s

'A night at the cinema was often finished off with a quick walk to the top of Bridgegate, to a fish and chip shop where they sold Bovril cakes. They were delicious and about the same size as a fishcake. We just had time to get some before running back to The Anchor pub to catch our bus home.'

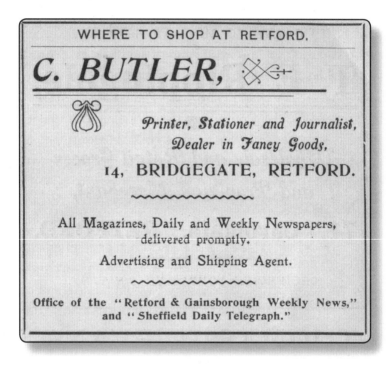

WHERE TO SHOP AT RETFORD.

C. BUTLER,

Printer, Stationer and Journalist,
Dealer in Fancy Goods,

14, BRIDGEGATE, RETFORD.

All Magazines, Daily and Weekly Newspapers,
delivered promptly.

Advertising and Shipping Agent.

Office of the "Retford & Gainsborough Weekly News,"
and "Sheffield Daily Telegraph."

Doug Davison

'It cost 4d to go to the cinema in the late 1920s and it cost about 2d for a few cigarettes which we smoked while watching the film. I would earn pocket money by doing a paper round before school. I collected the papers from Butler's shop on Bridgegate and did other odd jobs for them too like chopping wood and sweeping up.'

A young boy in the late 1920s

'On Saturday lunchtime, the Picture House on Carolgate was always packed with children, watching the Cowboy and Indian films. This lunchtime showing cost 1d and we got an orange too.

Sometimes I went roller-skating in the Butter Market. In the winter we went ice-skating on a lake in Babworth. When it was too dark to see, people with cars would put on their car headlights to shine on the lake.'

Skating

Babworth no longer has a lake. It is generally believed that subsidence caused by mining, (possibly at Bevercotes Pit) enabled the stream that fed the lake to find a different route. However, many Retfordians did skate there, especially in the harsh winters of the 1930s and 40s. The frozen lake, which belonged to the Whitaker estate, was checked for safety by someone dragging a heavy roller across the ice. If the ice was strong enough, a sign would be displayed to allow public skating.

The skate consisted of just a blade that screwed into the sole of the skaters boot with a leather toe strap over the top. In some winters, skating also took place on the canal between the locks.

Skating on Babworth Lake
(Welchman Collection)

'The winter of 1947 was very cold indeed. It was one of the coldest winters on record and Babworth lake froze solid........it was a pretty lake with an island in the middle which you could get to by crossing a rustic bridge.......... We even skated in the moonlight, and how lovely the forest looked, the trees glistening with frost and the skates gliding along on silver ice.'

Extract from *'Mulberries for Tea'* by Christine Crowther.

The Big Match

Fond memories of Cricket in Thrumpton
By George Roberts (born Thrumpton 1916)

One Friday night, on a summer's evening, sometime in the 1930s; there was a great feeling of excitement in the taproom of the New Inn in Thrumpton. The following day was to be the annual match between rival cricket teams, the Clinton Arms and the New Inn. The railway line divided the area into two with the lads from the New Inn on the southern side and the players that lived 'over the crossing' on the Clinton team.

The match would be the highlight of the local lads cricketing year and was the centre of conversation in the taproom on that particular Friday night.

The New Inn, Thrumpton Lane 2006

The match was to be played on a field next to the New Inn (which doubled as a football field in the winter months) with the River Idle running along the bottom.

Selecting a team was not usually a problem, but a bowler had to be carefully chosen. Fred, of course, would be the captain as he had prepared the wicket, (there would still be plenty of potholes). Jack was made wicketkeeper as he was the owner of a set of pads. It was known that the Clinton Arms also has a set of pads so that meant the keeper could wear a set and the batsmen would have one pad each. As Bill said, 'If you keep one leg behind the one with the pad on, you would come to no harm!'

Bill also thought that the team ought to dress a bit better than usual for this match but no-one had any whites and no-one could afford to buy them. By asking around, a few school caps were found for the occasion.
The umpire would have to be Ken, who could wear his white butcher's coat.

It has to be said that the track record of the team was not good as they had never won a match. They had drawn three, which they celebrated in style. On the day of this particular match, the sun was shining: it was going to be a great day for it.

The Clinton Arms 1920s.   (Welchman)

The Clinton Arms 2006

31

Everyone looked forward to the match. Wives would make tea and sandwiches which were taken when the batting side was out.

The rules of the game were carried out to the letter so at five minutes to two the umpires took to the field to inspect the wicket. After standing around talking about the weather for a few minutes, they gave the thumbs up to say that the game could begin.

The captains walked on to see who would bat first and the Clinton Arms won the toss. They chose to bat first. This meant that it was time for George to start swinging his arms around as he prepared to bowl. He didn't think that all this arm swinging did him much good but the pros did it, so he did too. George got ready to take his run; it was always a long one! As he walked out, a cry went up from the crowd 'Open the gate, he's going out the ground'.

The batsman took up his position with the umpire and the first ball was bowled.

George was not known for his accuracy and his first bowl was about a yard off the wicket. The umpire signalled a wide, but the lads were not too bothered and hopes were raised with the fourth ball, wide of the stumps, but the batsman made a move and the second slip caught it and a shout went up. Seeing as the ball was about a foot from the bat, the umpire had no hesitation in not giving an out, but it still gave the lads a bit of encouragement.

Now the sixth bowl was one that was talked about for years to come. George took his usual run. The ball bounced about nine inches off the wicket, hit a pothole and shot onto the stumps; 'clean bowled' went up the cry. By the time everyone had finished slapping George on the back, he was saying he had bowled 'off break'.

These weekend matches never produced big scores. If anyone scored more than five or six runs, the crowd got excited. The game went along slowly and all were out by catches. The bowlers were not known for hitting the wickets.

Towards the end of the match, the home team were getting anxious. They needed six runs to draw, seven to win. The last man to bat was Dick the blacksmith, a powerfully built man, but not a good batsman. His technique was to close his eyes and swing his bat and hope for the best! Down came the ball and Dick swung his bat and to everyone's surprise he hit the ball hard. Up went the ball, over the fence and into the next field. There had never been a six before and the umpire wasn't sure what sign to make, so he held up one hand and one finger on the other. After a few more bowls but no more score, the umpires were seen to converse and then called the match off on the grounds of 'bad light'. There was a small black cloud overhead but perhaps the umpires were just being diplomatic in creating a draw after a long game.

I remember these long ago days with great fondness as the community pulled together to make its own entertainment.

George Roberts 2006

School Holidays

The school holidays were filled with adventures and outdoor fun, with paper chases, swimming in the rivers and cycling for miles and miles until dusk.

Ken Sturgess, born on Century Road, was perhaps a little more adventurous than most. Ken and his friends discovered an explosives dump at Clumber Park during one of their bike rides. This was pure treasure to a young boy's scientific mind. Back in his father's shed, Ken experimented with the burning point of the explosives. All was going well until one particularly powerful blast shook the shed's foundations and removed Ken's eyebrows! Ken and the shed survived to continue their partnership in experiment and invention for many years to come.

Ken Sturgess

34

George Roberts and friends enjoyed paper chase games that covered many miles of the surrounding countryside. Two boys had to be chosen to lay the paper trail which was made of tiny pieces of newspaper. The torn up paper was stuffed into shoulder bags and the two trail-setters were given a head start. George's paper chase started from Thrumpton and went along Goosemoor Lane and out to Grove. The leaders would try to fool the following pack of boys by doubling back on their trail and of course the pack was aware of this and they tried to work out the tactics of the trail-setters. A good paper chase could take hours but George recalls arriving home exhausted but happy.

The swimming baths in Albert Road (built 1896) were very popular during the summer and often very crowded, but they usually closed in the winter.

Sign above the door of the Victorian Swimming Baths and Slipper Baths on Albert Road.

Children were taught to swim here. The popular method to encourage non-swimmers involved putting a rope around the child's middle and pulling him across the pool.

At the deep end of the pool were diving stages and along one side of the pool were chairs for spectators. When the attendants weren't looking, children would leap off the chairs into the water.

The Former Swimming Baths on Albert Road

Opposite the Albert Road swimming baths there is a small pocket park. After the First World War, a 'souvenir' tank rested there for many years and was a favourite piece of play equipment for local children, until it was removed, possibly for scrap during the Second World War.

The tank stood here for 20 years.
The swimming baths are in the background.

'Sherwood' the First World War Tank being taken to Albert Road *(Welchman)*

Conker collecting was popular in the autumn, just as it is now, but the annual conker tournament was a most serious event. George Roberts and his friends collected conkers in pillowcases from Mount Vernon, London Road, (in the 1930s, the home of Robert Eddison J.P.), then they carried their heavy load back home to share with friends in Thrumpton.

The collecting and swapping of cigarette cards was another very popular pastime. A long walk home from school was an ideal chance to play 'skimming'. Each child skimmed a cigarette card ahead of them and the owner of the card that went the furthest won the other cards. Another game involved standing some of the cards against a wall and each child flicked a card to try to knock one of the standing cards down.

There were hundreds of different cards to collect and the topics were often unusual such as *The Story of Sand, Poultry Rearing and By the Roadside*. With 25-50 cards in each set they were a great boost to the general knowledge of the children.

Then there was the building and the riding of trolleys, made from old pram wheels and wooden boxes. Riding down *'Gashouse Bridge'* (next to the Packet Inn) was a favourite track for Arthur Sanderson and there was very little traffic. Arthur also spent some of his school holidays, riding alongside a driver of the Co-op horse and dray. Deliveries of groceries were made to the local villages. As most families did not have a car, any chance to journey beyond the town was an adventure and Arthur enjoyed his packed lunch as he sat at the front of the dray. The Co-op also had its slaughter house on the corner of Nelson Street until larger premises were taken at the bottom of Blackstope Lane.

Potatoes being put into bags on Camm's Farm, Babworth.
Potatoes were stored in a large pile covered with straw known
as a potato pie.

(Sanderson)

Pocket Money

In the 1930's, pocket money was not readily given by parents, so the school holidays were a chance to earn a few bob (shillings) or pence, especially in the autumn when potato picking jobs were plentiful. Potato picking was tiring, back-breaking work, but farm trailers were always packed with willing workers from the town. Women and children would cycle several miles to a potato field, to be faced with a long cycle home again after a hard days work.

Potato picking on Camm's farm, Babworth

(Sanderson)

Tile pricking at the malthouses was tedious work but offered a few pence to children that were willing to take it on. The drying floor was made of earthenware tiles, under which were the kilns that provide the heat to dry the barley ready for the brewery. These earthenware tiles were coved in tiny holes to let the heat through to the grains of barley above. Some of the grains were small enough to block the pores of the tiles and youngsters were paid to lie on their tummies across the tiles and by using a sharp metal tool they poked out the grains from the holes; they were paid according to how many tiles they cleaned. Fred Pimperton took on this job when he was still at Thrumpton School and remembers his efforts to work very quickly to earn more pocket money. The malthouse where Fred was employed as a tile-pricker used to be south of the railway line on Thrumpton Road. Houses have been built on the site now but the photo below shows another, similar building on the same road.

Former Malt house, Thrumpton Lane

Between the ages of 12 and 14, Fred Pimperton worked part-time for Mudford's, the tent contractor. He usually worked in the school holidays and at weekends, but admits to sneaking in the occasional extra school day and hiding in a tent when school children went by. He enjoyed his work a great deal but did not know at the time how useful his tenting skills were going to be to the British Army in World War Two.

In 1941, Fred was in Egypt with the British Medical Corps. A hospital site was to be constructed on the edge of the desert. A few stone buildings were available on the site for use as a kitchen, operating theatre, etc., but about 1000 servicemen and women needed accommodation too. Large tents were delivered by lorries, but with no instructions. Fred came to the rescue with the knowledge and skills that he had learned from the men at Mudford's. He was put in charge of a team of thirty men and expertly showed them how to erect the huge tents.

Small amounts of pocket money could be earned by running errands for parents or neighbours. An errand might earn about 1d (less than 1p) but this would still be enough to buy a few sweets. The sweets that lasted the longest were the favourites, such as bulls-eyes and gobstoppers. George Roberts remembers standing outside the sweetshop for ages with 1d in his pocket, weighing up which selection of sweets was the best value for money.

A youngster in Ordsall might be lucky enough to get a weekend job at the golf course as golf players often hired young caddies. Walter Yowell, the local jeweller, played golf regularly and his young caddy would be well rewarded with at least 2/- (10p).

A sackful of acorns could be sold to a local pig farmer, but it took a lot of acorns to fill a sack, so this was done by a gang of children. Rosehips and crab-apples were collected in the autumn to make rosehip syrup and crab-apple jelly. Surplus jars of preserves could be sold to local shops such as the Co-op.

Working for farmers in the autumn was an official reason not to attend school. Work cards were issued to children that wanted time off school to work on farms during harvest time. The cards had to be signed and dated by the farmer to show that the child had used their day off for farm work.

> **"Whenever you are asked if you can do a job, tell'em 'Certainly I can' then get busy and find out how to do it"**
>
> *Theodore Roosevelt (1858-1919)*

The Best Football Field Ever

By George Roberts

When I talk to the eleven and twelve year olds today, they often tell me that they are bored and they don't know what to do. It made me think about what I used to do at that age in the school holidays.

In the 1920's there were no sports centres, not around here at any rate. Were we bored? No, never! One of the best pastimes for me was football. All the firms in the town had a team, so those were the games that we went to see as we had no money to go and see higher class games.
As we watched the local teams, we were fired up to play the game ourselves, but as there was no-one to organise us we had to do all the planning ourselves.

The first requirement was a field to play on, so we went to ask a local farmer if we could play in one of his nearby fields. We were delighted when he said yes, as long as we did no damage. As we sat on the fence inspecting our new pitch, we looked upon it as the best football field in the country. There were no goal posts of course or corner markings but a few coats would soon solve that problem. Billy thought, after inspecting it more closely, that it had more bumps than Mount Everest and thought that the farmer had let us have it in the hope that we might flatten it out a bit.

George Roberts

We hadn't got a ball, which was a bit of a problem. One of the lads called Jack had a father who kept the corner shop and Billy (the one with the brains) said that Jack's dad should buy us a ball as we had spent all our pocket money on sweets in his corner shop (tuppence per week each) so he must be rich. We eventually persuaded Jack to ask his dad for a ball. The suspense was terrible, but after two days Jack came along with a brand new football under his arm. Oh, the happy days we spent on our football field!

We needed to pick sides to make two teams so Jack became one of the captains (as he owned the ball) and Billy was the other one as it was his idea in the first place. We had no football boots or shirts but that didn't matter. We wore anything from hob-nail boots to stocking feet.

After a while, lads in the nearby streets heard about us and so they formed their team too. Many a hard fought match was played on that field. The only disputes were about whether a goal had been scored or not. Coats don't make ideal goal posts so decisions were made by the ref who was Jim, as he was the one with a watch and he could whistle loudly. No-one was left out and the little lad who had his legs in irons was our trainer. Where he got his bucket from, we shall never know but he was always there with his towel and water.

Our supporters were made up of two retired gentlemen. They were regular attendees and I'm sure that they enjoyed the sport as much as we did. At the end of the day we went home tired and happy and making plans for the next day.

This all took place on a field near to where the new Thrumpton School has been built and the farm was opposite where the school is. I started life 90 years ago at All Hallows Cottage, in Thrumpton and have many very happy memories of living there.

ACT OF GALLANTRY.

By courtesy of the " Notts. Weekly Guardian."
A.C.M. G. BREDDY.

George Breddy, a Retford A.C.M., has been awarded the Gilt Cross by the Chief Scout for his gallantry in rescuing a boy from drowning in the River Idle.

Breddy, with several other boys, had been bathing in the River Idle at a place known locally as The Butts. The river is generally shallow and slow-running, but at this place it is 6 to 8 feet deep and the current is rather swift. Breddy and most of the others had got out preparatory to getting dressed, when there was a cry that a boy was drowning. Breddy immediately ran to the bank where the boy was in difficulties (a matter of 100 yards), dived in and brought the boy to the bank, and administered artificial respiration. The boy was a poor swimmer, and had not Breddy had the presence of mind to jump in the river and get him to the bank, he might have been taken down by the current, which is very strong at this point. The boy could only swim a few strokes. No one helped Breddy until he got to the bank.

The following letter has been received from Imperial Headquarters:—

I am directed by the Chief Scout to forward for presentation to Mr. G. Breddy, Acting Assistant Cubmaster of the 8th Retford (St. Michael's) Group, the enclosed Gilt Cross in recognition of his gallantry in rescuing a boy from drowning in the River Idle, at Retford, on June 6th, 1933, and to ask that you will couple with its presentation the Chief Scout's congratulations and best wishes.

George Breddy rescued a boy from the River Idle and was awarded the Gilt Cross for his bravery. (see front cover)

47

SCHOOL DAYS

The first free Grammar School was built on Chapelgate in the 16th century. The London Road building of King Edward V1 Grammar School was opened in 1857. However, this fine institution only provided education for a small number of boys that either showed a scholarly aptitude or whose family was able to pay the fee.

Much of the schooling in Retford (as with most towns) relied heavily upon the churches, but even this was mainly for the education of boys.

In 1813 a National School was established on Chapelgate, followed by a larger National School on Grove Street in 1858, now known as St Swithun's. Several small private schools were also available in the town such as Miss Edna White's school at 17 Babworth Road.

Ordsall village school was originally opposite the Plough Inn on the High Street and the school at Thrumpton was known as the Retford Council School. Here, children could wear a cap embroidered with the initials R.C.S., which gave rise to the nickname, 'Retford Carrot Scrapers'!

Before the Secondary Modern Schools were built in the 1930s, many children went to the rather unglamorous looking Central School on Wharf Road, (where the fire station is now). The facilities at this site were limited, but one mischievous Retfordian can remember putting his hand through the railings to reach a couple of pieces of wood from the builder's yard next door, to use in a playground sword fight.

Ordsall Village School at it looks now.

Vic Hall recalls his schooldays in Ordsall from the 1930s.

'The school was staffed by the kindly Misses Thompson and Burton. There we learned the basics of education. We wrote on slates, drank our milk through real straws and the boys made raffia pictures while the girls learnt to knit.

The school stood at the junction of the High Street and Church Lane and often play was interrupted by a funeral procession when we had to be quiet and stand to attention. But what I remember about this little school, was the warm schoolroom in winter and its stove with the big fireguard, the visits at Christmas from the white bearded Father Christmas, who I realise in later years, was Mr Brett the verger, the school of course being a church school. But what I remember most was the joy of those days and the care shown to us by those two teachers who are sadly no longer with us.

And so I moved on with my contemporaries from Ordsall Infants to Thrumpton Council School where we moved upward year by year, segregated at playtime from the girls and split academically into classes A and B across the long school corridor, in the middle of which stood Mr Higgins' office, (the headmaster, with his sharp stinging cane) and at the end of which stood class 4A, taught by Mr Stansfield and where a few of us who had been selected to take the scholarship examination for entry to either the Grammar School for boys or the County High School for Girls, were given extra tuition by Mr Higgins, the headmaster.

The few who took the examination were selected on the basis of their parents' ability to pay for the school uniform, the sports gear, the leather satchel and all the other equipment considered necessary to put children on the route to a secure future. Most of those selected passed the examination and those who failed, if their parents could afford it, were admitted as fee payers.

The masters wore a cap and gown whilst teaching and the pupils had to dress smartly in school uniform and punctiliously obey the school rules. There was no caning and punishment was administered in the form of detentions or writing out the school rules, for which there was a lively black market.'

(Extract from *'Almost Forgotten'* by Vic Hall)

Ordsall School Children 1933   *(V.Hall)*

King Edward VI. Grammar School,
~~⟫ RETFORD. ⟪~~

Head Master   -   -   Rev. T. GOUGH, B.Sc., F.C.S.
Second Master   -   -   Mr. A. A. KIDSON, B.A., LL.B.
(With a Staff of Seven Assistant Teachers).

An Endowed School for Day Boys and Boarders, conducted on modern lines, with handsome buildings and complete equipment.

Prospectus on application to the Headmaster, or to—
Mr. T. H. DENMAN, Clerk to the Governors.

Margaret Morrell.

'I attended Lorne House School, which in the 1930's was next to the girls High School. During the war years we started school at 10am and left again at 3pm. I rode my bicycle to school from Babworth. Sometimes I went to school on my pony and left it in a relatives stable on Rectory Road until it was time to go home. If I didn't go to school by horse, it would be by bike. We would go everywhere by bike. One day I rode to town and left my bike in the Market Square while I went walking round. I was gone all afternoon but my bike was still there when I went back: no-one locked up their bike in those days.'

Lorne House, Queen Street 1930s   (Welchman)

Keith Smith

'I was taught in the Corn Exchange during the war. There were four classes in there and the huge room was divided up by four sheets of canvas. Our playground was the area that is now used as the Town Hall's car park, which at the time was a cattle market. We played among the railings at break time.'

Central School, Wharf Road, about 1930   (Welchman)

Thelma Larkinson

Thelma was evacuated to Retford from Yarmouth in 1940 and she attended the High School for Girls, now known as the Elizabethan High School. The lessons for the Yarmouth pupils and the Retford children had to be taken in shifts. As a Yarmouth girl, Thelma remembers taking a lesson between 8.30am and 9.50 and again between 2.50pm and 4.50. She also went to school on Saturday morning. The Retford pupils took their lessons in the time that was left between these shifts. Lesson times, however, did vary, as sometimes another building became available, such as Glenesk, the large house near the railway footbridge off Queen Street (now a nursing home).

Lunch time could be fun as it was often eaten in the floating dining room! Sandwiches brought from home would be eaten on a barge moored alongside the High School.

Boys wore short trousers until they went to the secondary school and their socks were held up by two straps. Poverty was commonplace during the war years and children were often poorly dressed, especially in winter. When shoes were not available, the child did not go to school. It was a full time task for the school attendance officer (school bobby) to chase absentees.

Paper was very precious and children were instructed to use every inch of the page, even the margin. Electricity was saved by schools voluntarily turning off their heating for some of the day and it was a common sight in the National School, (now St Swithun's), to see children and staff sitting in their coats to keep warm.

Thelma recalls that Retford took part in the County's 'Education Week' during the late 1940s and that Retford came out as one of the best towns in the county. Every organisation in the town was encouraged to stage events, such as sport and drama, that would involve the whole community and the townsfolk of Retford entered into the spirit of this with enthusiasm.

Royal Wave

The smallest unexpected moment can sometimes make the most treasured memory. This happened to two young Retford boys one day after school. A father of one of the boys was a railwayman and had heard that a train arriving in Retford would have a royal coach attached. The two boys ran to the goods yard for the 4 o'clock train from London. As the steam train slowly pulled out of the station, the two end coaches with curtains came into view and to the boys' delight the curtains were open and they could clearly see Queen Mary in her carriage wearing one of her familiar large hats. The schoolboys raised their caps to her and to their delight the Queen waved back.

Queen Mary

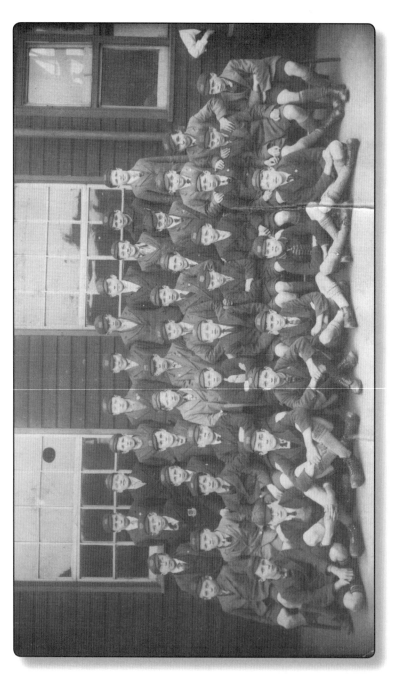

Central School, Wharf Road   (Roberts)

58

EBB AND FLO

Two local characters that lived on the roads.

Ebb and Flo were local characters, remembered by everyone that lived in the town in the 30s and 40s. It is generally accepted that Ebb was Herbert Fletcher from Manton Hall who fell in love with Florence, a maid. The pair was inseparable and chose a life of travelling the roads between Retford and Worksop, although sometimes they brought back stories from further afield.

Children were heard shouting abuse at the couple and it was usual for Ebb and Flo to hurl verbal abuse back, however, many Retfordians have fond memories of the couple.

Keith Smith

'I moved to Retford from Doncaster. One of my earliest memories is a journey that my family made from Doncaster to Retford. We were travelling back from Doncaster and we took the right turn after the Old Bell Hotel. This road takes you over a small bridge which crosses the canal. As we approached the bridge we could see two people sitting on it, one on either side. They had their backs against the sides of the bridge with their legs stretched out in front of them. As we got nearer, the two people had to pull their legs in to let the car pass. I remember turning round to look out of the back window to get a better view of these two characters. One was a man, wearing a battered trilby. His hair was sticking out from underneath it and he had quite a good sized beard. The other person was a woman. Both of them had layers and layers of clothing on, tied round the middle with string. I learnt later that these two folk were locally known as Ebb and Flo. They had no fixed address and seemed to spend their entire life wandering between Retford and Worksop.

One day, me and some friends were on a bike ride, going towards Sandy Lane, near Ranby. We could see smoke coming up from near the huts at Ranby Camp. When we reached the source of the smoke we found Ebb and Flo sitting on ammunition boxes; they were cooking lunch on a make shift camp-fire.

Ebb and Flo would push all they owned around in an old pram. When Flo broke her leg, she was pushed around in this pram by Ebb'.

June Smith

June Smith met Flo, when Flo was admitted to hospital. On arrival, Flo was very dirty and unkempt but when we had bathed her, she was beautiful with lovely fair hair.

'I used to talk to her about Retford and she was very fond of Ordally (Ordsall). Ebb had permission to see her any time; we screened them off from the other patients. Ebb would be given a mug of cocoa and some cheese sandwiches. He thanked us by selling us his copy of Old Moores Almanac.'

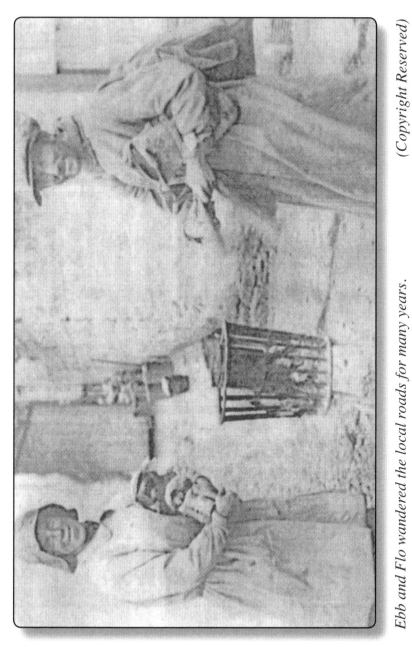

Ebb and Flo wandered the local roads for many years.

Fred Pimperton

'I met Ebb and Flo many times but especially Ebb. When I was a nurse at the hospital in Kilton, Ebb was admitted due to a mild illness. He desperately needed a bath and it was my job to help him. He didn't mind getting undressed but he wouldn't let go of his leather money bag. It was a big money bag like the ones a bus conductor used to use. He wouldn't put it down even when he was in the bath so he sat there holding the bag over the side.

Ebb and Flo were always on the move. Some nights they would sleep in a bus shelter or a farmer's barn. When I cycled to work from Retford to Kilton hospital, I would see them asleep in a bus shelter at Ranby. Sometimes Flo would get in the pram and Ebb would push her along.

Before meeting Ebb and Flo, I had already met many local travellers and homeless people because, just after the Second World War, I worked in the Spital Hill workhouse, (Hillcrest Nursing Home as it was known by then). There were about a dozen men and a dozen women. The men and women lived in separate sections. Sometimes a traveller would come by and he just wanted a bed for the night and some food. To get this he would have to do half a days work at the workhouse such as washing pots or gardening. There were at least six people that were so frail that they were permanently in bed.

One chap that arrived had been kicked by a racehorse and he was seriously injured. He gave me a tip to put money on Tommy Weston's horse. I never had enough money to risk on betting so I didn't place the bet but I wish I had because the horse won the race and the odds were 10-1.'

WAR TIME

Memories of the War Years (1939-1945)
Written by J.A.J

I was born in 1931 at Thrumpton, East Retford, so by the time the Second World War started in 1939, I was at that age of acute curiosity and aware of all that was happening around me. My memories of this era are still very vivid in my mind to this day. The events described below are just a fragment of what was happening during those eventful years.

The declaration of the outbreak of war with Germany didn't seem to have a great deal of effect upon young children, apart from noticing that parents showed great interest in the news bulletins which were broadcast on the radio. It was only when we noticed strange things starting to happen in Retford that we realised that something was going to start affecting us personally. For instance, I remember my father bringing home a roll of brown sticky paper about one inch wide and he proceeded to cut it into strips and stick it diagonally across all the window panes. When I asked him what it was for I was told that if a bomb fell outside the house, it would stop the windows from breaking into small pieces and injuring us inside.

Over the next few days I noticed that all our neighbours had the same fears and had stuck the sticky paper on their windows too. Not long after, some bricklayers arrived and they built a seven foot high wall along the entire backs of all the houses, just feet away from the rear windows. We were told it was a blast wall and was a protection against bomb blast. It certainly altered the outlook at the rear of the house.

On another occasion, we witnessed two men pushing a handcart with two steel bottles on it. We found out later they were oxy acetylene bottles and anyone fortunate enough to own ornamental railings at the front of their properties would soon be without them. We were told they were going away to be made into guns and tanks.

Even schools did not escape from the threat of wartime. Everyone was issued with gas masks which we had to carry at all times in case the Germans sent over a gas attack. These masks were kept in square cardboard boxes with a string attached to put across your shoulders for ease of carrying. Those who preferred, could buy proper tin boxes to carry the masks. I did notice that after the knocking and banging about they usually received at playtimes, you could see a residue of charcoal in the bottom of the tin, which could I suppose have rendered the gas mask less effective.

One of the lighter sides of having a gas mask was the regular practise of making us wear them whilst in the classroom at school. This was to get us used to wearing them in case of a real attack. When we tried to talk to each other it was virtually impossible to understand what the others were saying. Also, as breath was being expelled they made the most frightful rude noise which did not help the discipline of the classroom. After all those years I still retain the memory of the smell of the rubber and the feeling of perspiration that collected on my face after a few minutes of wearing them.

Wartime Vehicle on Bridgegate near the corner with Hospital Road 1939   *(Welchman)*

Another vivid memory of those war time school days concerned a local plane crash. On this occasion, word quickly circulated around the classes that one of our aircraft, a bomber, had crashed in Babworth Wood, killing all the crew. At the first opportunity nearly every pupil at the school was heading for Babworth Wood to see that crashed plane before the RAF salvage crews carted it away.

St John's Ambulance Brigade on parade.
St Swithun's Church 1939

(Pimperton)

Of course, it was our aim to try and find a piece of the aircraft, to take away as a souvenir. This task was relatively easy as the aircraft had disintegrated on impact and scattered debris over a large area of the woods. The RAF crash guards, sent to the wreck, could not have possibly kept control of all the children wandering through the woods.

A few days later, there arrived at our classroom, a police officer who announced that he knew we had all been to Babworth Woods. He said that he was also aware that items had been removed from the site, which was a very serious matter, and that if the items could be recovered, nothing more would be said. If not, we would all have to be placed under arrest! This last statement triggered a barrage of scraping chairs and banging of desk lids, followed by a stampede to the front with arms full of ill gotten booty. The table at the front of the classroom soon creaked under the weight of live ammunition belts, hundreds of live cartridges, chunks of aluminium, pipe work, cables, and strange objects that no one could identify. I did notice that it took the policeman several trips to empty the table.

During the war years there were many plane crashes in the area. It became a challenge to try and acquire, by fair means or foul, a piece of the cockpit window as these were made from plastic called Perspex. As small boys, this was a very desirable commodity to own. If one had a penknife, a small file and a bit of sandpaper, the Perspex could be cut and filed into jewellery, the most popular being signet rings. After hours of cutting, filing and polishing with Brasso, a very presentable item was the end product. I sadly mislaid or lost my collection many years ago.

Another lasting memory is the air raid sirens. They had two distinct sounds. The first being a warning of an impending raid, this one had a tone that went up and down. The second tone was the "all clear" which stayed at a constant pitch. If we were at school and the siren sounded, we would be led by the teachers down into the concrete shelters situated around all schools. You can still see the remains of one of these shelters if you go down Domini Cross Road to the rear of what was the Grammar School. It has been shortened considerably, but one can still see its form of construction. These shelters had rows of wooden benches down each side, the pupils sat in two rows facing each other. The shelters were cold, dark and damp and smelt very musty. The only light source being a storm lantern held aloft by the teacher in charge. There you sat, until the "all clear" sounded.

If the air raid warning siren sounded out of school hours, your actions relied upon your family's resourcefulness. Some families, but not many in this area had dug shelters in their gardens, covering them over with corrugated iron, with earth piled on top. Others had bought indoor shelters built like a big square metal cage, and covered in strong steel netting. The one I remember was in the local doctor's surgery waiting room and when it was not in use as a shelter, it served as a table. My parents did what most families did in the area, and that was to go under the stairs when the sirens sounded, which happened mostly at night. It had been noticed by the authorities that many bombed houses still had the stairs standing after the rest of the building had collapsed. We fortunately never saw it put to the test, but I remember we spent many hours under the stairs, which also doubled as a pantry.

What one must realise, although Retford was not a strategic target for bombing, it was directly on the flight path of the German raiders heading for Sheffield which was a major target because of the steel works and industrial areas there. When in residence under the stairs during a raid, you could always tell if the plane overhead was a German bomber or one of ours, just by listening to the engines. The enemy plane engines had a peculiar uneven beat which my father said was down to bad workmanship. Years later we found out that the German aircraft used to desynchronise their engines to try and avoid our radar systems finding them.

Another means of locating them was by search lights, if you were brave enough to venture outside at night during a German raid, you could see intense bright beams poking up into the sky, looking for enemy aircraft with the intention of showing the anti-aircraft section where to aim their guns, hopefully to shoot the raider down. During the war there was a search light unit in the playing field down Bracken Lane.

My father joined the local Home Guard, and when he wasn't working, he went out at night to guard something or other. I remember him coming home dressed in his khaki uniform and carrying a rifle, although I can never remember him having any bullets.

Another role carried out by civilians was that of Air Raid Warden. His duty was to patrol the streets of Retford at night looking for people showing bits of light through the curtains after dark. This was because, throughout the war years, it was forbidden to show any light after dark in case a bomber could see it. No street lamps could be lit either. The blackout went on for about four years. It was a most strange feeling after the war when all the lights in Retford were switched back on again.

As I come to the end of my reminiscences I must mention the street parties. These were to celebrate the end of the war in Europe, VE day (Victory in Europe).
Most streets had parties, with benches and tables stretching across the streets, decorated with home made bunting and flags stretching from house to house. I went to a party held in South Street, and it was amazing what the women-folk managed to produce, even though they had been on severe food rationing for the last four years. We had jelly and cake and it tasted wonderful but I can't imagine now what ingredients they used because we never normally had any fancy food. I can honestly say that it was the happiest and the very best party I have even been to.

JAJ 2006

Keith Smith

'War was announced to me when I was 14 years old from the pulpit of St Michael's church. We all left church that day feeling very subdued. I felt dreadful and bewildered, not knowing what was going to happen.'

A Midnight Caper

Wartime created new, responsible roles for some sixth form pupils at King Edward VI School. Each night a group of four boys would be on 'fire watch' which would earn them 1/- (5p). A dark empty school was a tempting place for a bit of mischief and one night two boys decide to explore the building, making an unofficial inspection of the loft.

At that time the headmaster lived on the premises and the sound of movement overhead came to his attention. Up above in the loft, the two boys came upon a trapdoor which they lifted, only to be confronted by the headmaster standing below in his dressing gown, brandishing a golf club and flash light. The boys bid a hasty retreat back to their room and when a policeman arrived, they denied all knowledge of the incident!

The Retford Spitfire

In 1940, the people of Retford and District began fund-raising to purchase a presentation spitfire at a cost of £5000, to be donated to the Royal Air Force. The effort from the community was outstanding with all societies, families and pubs getting involved with concerts, knitting groups and even a 'mile of pennies'. The Retford Cricket ground exhibited a Messerschmitt fighter which had been shot down. Money received from this exhibition also went to the Retford Spitfire Fund

Large, private donations were made too and within just four months the target amount had been raised. A photograph of the plane bearing the name 'Retford and District' and the Retford coat of arms can be seen in *'Jiri: the Story of a Spitfire' by Vic Hall*.

Albert Hall

The small mission hall on Albert Road was set up as a soldiers' rest room during the war, although it was never used for this purpose. It was, however, regularly used as a place of worship as it was easier to 'black out' than the large Methodist church on Grove Street.

Albert Hall, Albert Road 2006

OFF TO WORK

The history of the town's workplaces could surely fill a book of its own. Retford was once known for its vibrant and prosperous manufacturing industries, such as sail cloth making, rope making (especially steel rope), rubber products, textiles, and paper to name a few. Family businesses were once the foundation of the prosperity of the town. Some family businesses are long standing and against all odds have survived the 1930's depression and the 1980's recession.

The following chapter is about the workplaces that the contributors to this book experienced for themselves and therefore it covers a limited number of shops and industries in the town during the first half of the 20th century.

The Northern Rubber Company

Ernest Widdowson was born in 1908 and started work at The Northern Rubber Company in 1925 as an office boy in the textile division. He continued to work with the company until he retired from his post as Chief Clerk to the Textile Division in 1975. This is his own account of one of Retford's oldest manufacturing industries. (First published in the *Retford and District Historical and Archaeological Society's Annual Review 2002*)

'The company was founded in 1871 by Mr. Alfred Pegler who adapted a small factory in Victoria Street to rubber manufacturing, which had previously been used for making a type of linoleum.

For many years the offices were situated in old houses and following extensions to the Mechanical factory up to about 1930, the old properties were pulled down and new laboratories built.

Ernest Widdowson

Some time later, a row of houses on Thrumpton Lane were demolished to make way for new offices, bringing the directors and main staff of the Mechanical and Textile divisions together. Both divisions of the Company continued to operate independently. I have been connected with the Textile division for almost 50 years, after joining as an office junior in 1925. At that time the Company employed about 600 people, men and women. In many cases several members of the same families.

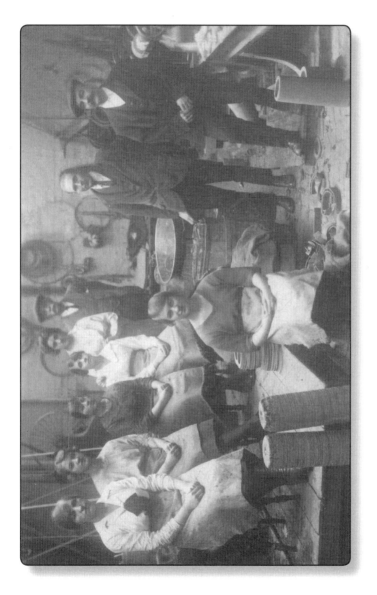

The Moulding Room. The Northern Rubber Company. 1920s (Sanderson)

One member of staff was employed full time dealing with Spanish business; he would spend six months each year in Spain. He was quite a character and one of the older generation. Short in stature, his legs would dangle from his seat on a high stool; he conversed little with anyone, but mainly with himself. He would write his letters, which were placed into a book containing flimsy paper and a damp pad, then into a very large press to leave the imprint of correspondence. A few years later, the offices moved into the old clinic, which was adjacent; this allowed more space for storage of goods in the hospital. Eventually as already mentioned, new offices were built at the factory, members of staff were transferred and the stocks of cloth etc. were removed to a section of the Textile factory. Following the move to new offices the old building was taken over by the Whitehall Youth Centre. More recently it was demolished to make way for house building.

So far as Textile products are concerned, I will try to recollect the main types being produced, through the years to my retirement. Going back to the years prior to 1939, about half of the total production was destined for export to China. It was the most expensive garment material produced at the time. This had to be packed in tin lined cases, four rolls to a case. A man from Gyles, the ironmongers in Grove Street at that time, would come to solder the tin lids down.

RETFORD

IS AN IDEAL PLACE FOR

MANUFACTURERS

BECAUSE

 IT IS IN THE CENTRE OF ENGLAND.

 Goods put on Rail can be delivered next morning at all the Principal Towns.

 Of its abundant and CHEAP WATER SUPPLY.

 Of its CHEAP GAS for MOTOR POWER.

 Of its LOW RATES.

 SUITABLE LAND can be had at REASONABLE PRICES.

Further particulars may be had from

W. P. JONES, Esq., Town Clerk.

About that period, the Company was producing motor hooding materials; both embossed leather cloth and double texture types. During the late 1930s, the Company decided to mass produce lightweight coated fabrics for the waterproof garment trade. Most of that production was purchased by firms in Manchester and London for making up into cheap mackintoshes for Marks and Spencer, selling at 5/- each, (25p).

By 1930, the Company was producing a greater yardage of coated rubber textiles than any of our competitors in the country.

At this time, a large warehouse in Manchester was taken over to store both cloth and coated materials. A vehicle would transport coated supplies several times weekly, returning with cloth. The company also had their own garment making department when I arrived in 1925, which found work for about forty people, women and men. Many of the better class garments were supplied to large London stores for school uniforms, also to Police forces and Railway Companies. From 1939, the priority was for materials intended for the War effort; some going into munitions, also a large quantity of groundsheet capes were supplied. I suppose new types were developed during the period when I was away for four years in the RAF. More recently, the company decided to commence production of heavier types of materials, for the shopping bag trade, etc. Substantial yardages were involved of various types, most supplied to makers-up in this country. Still more recently, heavily coated synthetic fabrics went into production for use in the making of hovercraft skirts. The material was transported to Cowes in the Isle of Wight. Hospital sheeting of various weights was produced right down the years. I recollect some of this being shipped to Archangel in northern Russia during the war, about 1941, by convoy of course. Some very lightweight synthetic fabrics were coated in special compounds for use in the aircraft industry. In fact, Northern Rubber materials were used in Concorde. Very many other applications for rubber coated fabrics served various industries, such as camera bellows.

Beyond the Textile factory, close to the river bank was a small building, where about six people, mainly women, were employed making hot water bottles, surgical gloves, air cushions and air beds. When production was discontinued after very many years, new operating plants were installed to manufacture imitation suede; many thousands of yards over a number of years, being shipped mainly to Singapore, Hong Kong and Australia.

It later became necessary to turn to new products, the impregnation of fabric and cutting into strips for vertical blinds, also back-coating of upholstery materials. A percentage of various coated materials were always being supplied to the mechanical factory, going into the making of components for the engineering industry. The company had a number of representatives covering Britain, in addition to Agencies, and Associated Companies, overseas.
It was a rather sad occasion for me to witness the end of the Textile Factory after so many years of service.'

The Northern Rubber Works, Thrumpton Lane.

Fred Pimperton

Fred Pimperton started work with the Northern Rubber Company when he left school in 1931. He was kept busy, cleaning up the garment room where he watched diving suits being made by Harry Smedley. Later, he moved into the spreading room where fabric was made waterproof by being coated with a layer of rubber. A gentleman's raincoat was displayed in a town centre shop with water being sprayed over it to show the effectiveness of this waterproofing method.

A Fourteen Year Old Errand Boy

'My first job was in the bakery on Grove Street called Howard's Bakery. At the age of 14 (in 1936) I was an errand boy and worked six days a week for 6 shillings and 9 pence, (about 34p). The hours were long, often from 8am to 8 pm. If I worked late I didn't get any extra money. In those days you were just pleased to have a job.

I would often have to ride out to the villages to deliver bread or milk. I remember cycling all the way out to Eaton Hall with just a carton of cream in my bicycle basket. The bike had an oil lamp for dark evenings in the winter and I would be sent on errands in all weathers. If the shop got a phone call from Welham Hall for a Hovis loaf, I would be sent on my bike to take it straight away. When I wasn't running errands I would be at the back of the bakery, greasing the baking sheets and tins ready for the bakers the next morning. I also had to rake out the ashes from the bread ovens ready for fresh fuel to be put in.

Out of my 6/9d wages, I would give 6/- to my mother for the housekeeping and keep 9d for myself. 9d lasted me most of the week: there wasn't much to spend it on.

I later became a delivery boy with Wards, the beer and soft drinks distributor that were based in Retford. I worked five and a half days for them and earned 10 shillings (50p) a week. Ward's distributed beer from the Swinton brewery and Smiths crisps. A delivery to Lincoln by van would take nearly half a day and it was my job to start the van each time with the crank handle.

Much later, after the Second World War, I worked on the Retford railway, cleaning engines. I started there as a trainee fireman which meant that I learnt to look after the fires that fuelled the steam engines.

The hours of work were a bit strange as I sometimes started work at 1.15am and a caller from the railway would come to my house to wake me up by tapping on the bedroom window with a long pole.

As a fireman I earned £3 a week and I was given three pairs of overalls. My best memory in this job was when I got the chance to fire the Mallard from Retford to Peterborough. The train had pulled into Retford and the fireman on duty had to get off due to illness. I was at the station on standby at the time (sitting in a signal box) and I was called to take over. It was a thrill to fire the Mallard and I was sorry to have to get off at Peterborough to catch a train back to Retford.'

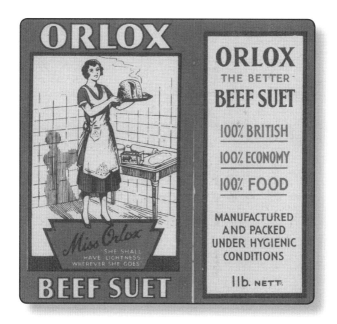

Front cover of a box of Orlox beef suet

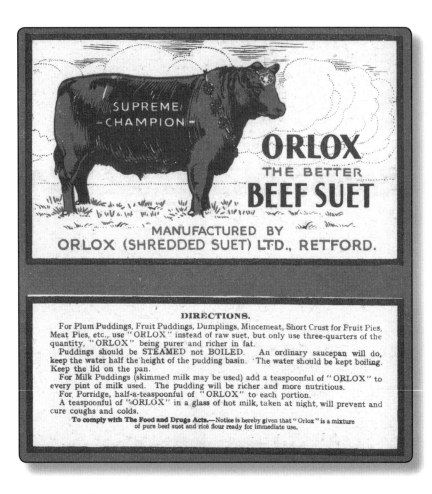

Orlox claimed to be a cough and cold remedy.
Orlox Ltd, 9 Cannon Square.

MARKETS AND SHOPS

In 1936, there were 9 butchers' shops on Carolgate alone. There were 7 confectioners (not including newsagents and tobacconists) and 6 greengrocers and streets such as New Street and West Street offered a great variety of trades.

Shop Assistant 1948

'When I was 16 years old I started work at Dickman and Fletchers, the department store on Carolgate. I was interviewed by Mrs Dickman. She was a tall, smartly dressed lady and her hair was always perfectly done. She asked me about my work in the village shop where I had worked previously. I was so nervous because Fletchers was a huge shop compared with a village post office. I got the job and started on £1 per week in 1948. It cost me 4 shillings a week to travel to work, that's about 20p nowadays, and I had to go in 6 days a week although I had Wednesday afternoon off because it was half day closing. On this half day off I would go to Worksop to look round the shops and the market and on Thursday (the half day closing in Worksop) the Worksop shop girls would come to Retford.'

"I base my fashion taste on what doesn't itch"

Gilda Radner (1946 - 1989)

The Children's department, in 'Dickman and Fletchers' shop.
1-3 Carolgate.1940s

(Welchman)

When I could quote all the prices of goods by heart, my wage went up to one pound, three shillings and sixpence, which would be less than £1.20 nowadays. On top of this I could earn commission on sales but this didn't happen very often at first because each sales assistant had an order of seniority and I was 'third sale' to start with so I had to wait until my two senior colleges were serving customers before I got a chance. Sometimes the customers would tell me that they wanted to wait for Miss Wagstaff because they had come for nylon stockings. Stockings were still on ration after the war and a small quantity were kept under the counter but I wasn't allowed to sell them because they were reserved for 'special' customers!

At the start of the day it was my job (along with two other girls) to sweep the front of the shop and remove the bars from the windows. Apart from a lunch break we would get a 10 minute break and we were given a drink of cocoa. This was just after the war and the cocoa tasted nothing like as nice as the sort you get today.

My extra duty each week was to go round the whole department store and collect a penny off everyone so that we could buy toilet paper. Some of the girls that lived in town complained that they didn't use the shop toilet and shouldn't have to pay!

We had to wear all black clothing except for a little white collar. By the mid 1950's I was in charge of the children's clothing department and my pay had risen to £3 per week and I got one week holiday with pay.

June Smith

'In the 1940s, at the age of 14, I started work in a ladies outfitters known as Miss Best (72 Carolgate). In good weather, I would cycle 7 miles to work, and park my bike at the back of the shop. I never locked it up.

Miss Best's shop sold pure wool, pastel shades were plentiful, but khaki and grey were not, as so much was being used for socks and gloves for soldiers in the war. This wool would be reserved for regular customers. I was a very shy 14 year old and one particular customer used to scare me to death. She always wore a long back coat and a pull on "cloche" hat and boots.

She was as thin as a straw. If she asked me for khaki wool I could only let her have 1oz. If she saw me in the street, she would curse me and throw obscenities in for good measure – what a lady! I can also remember heavily pregnant ladies coming to the shop to buy baby wool and it amused me how they would rest their large tummies on the counter! These ladies were often from Eaton Hall which was used during the war as a maternity home for pregnant ladies evacuated from Sheffield.

At Miss Best's, we also sold corselettes, laced roll-on corsets and suspender belts. Gossard and Spirella were the main makes. We also sold the most beautiful underwear such as pure silk underskirts with French knickers to match. Also, loose fitting cami-knickers trimmed with lace, under which you were supposed to wear ordinary knickers, but we never did. Then there was, (the not so glamorous) E.T.B's (elastic top and bottom). Some were huge, with a kite gusset, which meant that the gusset went from the very back of the knickers to the front waist band. They were made of stretchy cotton called lock-knit. We also sold lots of Winciette nighties and pyjamas. We sold pure silk stockings, but during the war and the years of rationing, these were only sold to Miss Best's friends. Other stockings were very thick, and had a back seam. A cherished Christmas gift would be a pair of fur gloves or mittens; men came in the shop to buy these for their wives and girlfriends. In the 1940s, ladies could buy cotton "Double 2" long sleeved blouses. These came with a collar attached and a spare collar. There were also Viyella dresses and blouses which always creased.

Advertisement in "Homeland Handbook"

We sold Fair Isle, pure wool, jumpers, waistcoats and cardigans. The cardigans were only waist length in those days.

During rationing, most clothes bore a utility label at the back of the neck. One weekend, we had a burglary at the shop and the burglars cut off all the labels and threw them on the floor. A burglary was almost unheard of in those days, so this was quite scandalous.

The shop opened between 9 and 6pm and closed at 1pm on Wednesdays. At about 5.45 pm, I would scatter damp sawdust on the lino floor and then sweep it up. The sawdust was used to stop the dust on the floor flying everywhere.'

June Smith and Muriel Ogle

Muriel Ogle

'After leaving school, I started work in Sterling's shoe shop (9 Carolgate). Most of the morning was taken up with cleaning and polishing. The windows were cleaned with just water and a leather cloth. The floor was polished with hard wax polish, making it a perfect surface for small boys to slide around on.

The managers in those days expected the sale assistants to try their hardest to secure a sale. If the manager could hear that a customer was starting to lose interest, they would come along and take over the sales pitch and invariably secure the sale.

In good weather I cycled to work from Torworth (about 5 miles) which saved me 6d out of my £2 a week pay.

I later moved to Dewhursts, the butcher (8 Carolgate), into the office. Dewhursts supplied meat to all the schools in portions according to the rationing regulations. Meat was also supplied to Rampton Hospital and Headon Camp.'

Sterlings Shoe shop. 9 Carolgate.   (Welchman)

Eating Out

A shopping trip to Retford in the 1940s might include a visit to one of the restaurants or refreshment rooms. The word 'café' was occasionally used but often pronounced 'caff'. The tea rooms at Howard's on Grove Street were popular and were on two floors, where the fresh smell of baking was very inviting as everything was made on the premises.

First floor tea room, Howard's café. The stairs in the background led to a tea room on the next floor.

(Welchman)

The British Restaurant on Wharf Road was described as 'cheap and cheerful', where a good quality two course meal could be bought for about 1/- (5p) in the 1940s. The building was situated where the fire station is now and was made from wood with a corrugated metal roof. The food was traditional such as minced beef and vegetables followed by old fashioned pudding such as 'spotted dick' bread and butter pudding or jam roly poly.

Near to the British Restaurant was a day nursery that was used by mothers doing war work. It was for babies and children up to school age. June Smith helped at the nursery on Wednesday afternoons which was her half day off from shop work. She can remember the noise of the voices of up to 60 children at play. In the afternoon, small metal beds were pulled out so that the smallest children could have a nap, after which the babies had their nappies changed and were given a drink of blackcurrant juice.

Howard's Bakery, Grove Street 1935.   *(Welchman)*

Suggested further reading.

- The Book of Retford. James Roffey.
  (Bookworm of Retford).

- Ornament of Sherwood Forest, J. Fletcher.
  (Country Books)

- Views of Old Retford.
- North Nottinghamshire from the Air
- Life in Wartime Bassetlaw
  (Retford Historical and Archaeological Society)

- Almost Forgotten. Vic Hall

- Old Retford (postcards) David Ottewell.
  (Stenlake Publishing)

- Images of England–Retford and the Bassetlaw Area
  Peter Tuffrey. (Tempus Publishing)

- Jiri: The Story of Spitfire R7218. Vic Hall.
  (Country Books)

- Retford in Old Picture Postcards
  (Reflections of a Bygone Age)

- Further photographs from the Welchman Collection can
  be viewed at Bassetlaw Museum, Amcott House, Grove
  Street, Retford., and on the website,
  www.bassetlawmuseum.org.uk